START-A-CRAFT

Stencilling

Get started in a new craft with easy-to-follow

projects for beginners

BETSY SKINNER AND JAMIE SAPSFORD

APPLE

A QUINTET BOOK

Published by The Apple Press
6 Blundell Street
London N7 9BH

ISBN 1-84092-016-5

This book was designed and produced by
Quintet Publishing Limited
6 Blundell Street
London N7 9BH

Creative Director: Richard Dewing
Designer: Ian Hunt
Senior Editor: Laura Sandelson
Editor: Lydia Darbyshire
Photographer: Chas Wilder

Typeset in Great Britain by
Central Southern Typesetters, Eastbourne
Manufactured in Hong Kong by
Regent Publishing Services Limited
Printed in China by Leefung-Asco Printers Trading Ltd

NOTE

Contents

Introduction

Welcome to the joys of stencilling!

Start-a-Craft Stencilling will take you on a simple, step-by-step guided tour of 13 projects, and by the time you reach the end of this book you will have experienced the wonderful and creative world of stencilling and all it offers.

A stencil is simply a design shape cut out of a piece of wax card, thin metal or plastic film. When paint is applied through the cut-out, the shape is reproduced on the surface below.

Stencilling is not a modern craft. It has been used for centuries as a means of decorating fabrics, books, pottery and of course, the home itself. Early examples can still be seen in homes and museums all over the world, especially in the USA. When expensive European wallpapers were imported to the USA in the 19th century, most people could not afford to buy them. The designs provided stencil artists with new inspiration, and the art of stencilling meant that the effects of the wallpaper could be imitated at a fraction of the cost of the real thing.

Eventually, mass-production meant that even the expensive wallpapers were within the reach of most people, and stencilling lost its popularity. However, in recent years, as people have looked for new ways to bring individuality to their homes, stencilling has come back into fashion.

The projects in this book explore the versatility of the craft. They range from a very simple yet effective gift tag, through more complicated items to the challenge of designing your own stencil. The projects have been planned to allow you to develop your knowledge and skills of stencilling in a gradual way, so that when you have mastered one technique you will have the confidence to move on to more creative, demanding things. Each project includes extra ideas to inspire you and helpful tips to enable you to produce professional-looking stencils.

The materials you will need can usually be found at your local art shop or do-it-yourself store, and you can also buy a wide variety of ready-made stencils. If you want to make your own stencils, see Designer's Delight (see page 40), which covers designing and cutting. A selection of our designs can be found in the pattern library at the back of the book.

So, let's go! All you have to do is gather your tools and materials together, follow the projects in this book, and you can take part in the revival of this appealing and rewarding craft.

Happy stencilling!

Jamie Sapsford and Betsy Skinner
The Bermuda Collection

Materials and Equipment

PAINTING KIT
You will need some or all of these materials:

Ready-made Stencils
There is a wide choice available, but do consider the size, shape and intricacy of a design when you are deciding what would be most appropriate for a particular project.

Stencil Brushes
Thick bristled brushes are used to apply paint through the stencil, and they are available in a variety of sizes. A good range to start would be sizes 4, 8, 12 and 16.

Low-tack Masking Tape
You must make sure that the stencil lies flat in place for painting, and low-tack tape reduces the risk of damaging your work surface, such as a wall. Spray adhesive is an alternative for fixing your stencil temporarily in place.

Stencil Paints
Artist's acrylics can be applied to most surfaces. Fabric paints should be used for fabrics, and special paints are available for use on ceramics and glass. Use fast-drying paints to avoid smudging problems during layering. Water-based paints are easier to clean up.

Bowls
Old, small china bowls are useful for mixing colours, and they are easy to clean.

Paper Kitchen Towel
This is essential for general cleaning up and for removing excess paint from your brush.

Scrap Paper
Have plenty of scrap paper handy so that you can practise.

Ruler
Always have a ruler for measuring and placing your stencils.

RIGHT
Painting materials.

Scissors

Apart from trimming some of the papery projects, you will need a pair of scissors for dozens of other uses.

Pencil, Sharpener and Rubber Eraser

Finally, make sure your pencil is sharp so that you always cut along a clean line.

> After every project, clean up when you have finished and wash out your brushes and stencils made of polyester with soap and warm water.

CUTTING KIT

Polyester Drafting Film

This is excellent material for making your own stencils. The frosted transparent film is easy to draw on and perfect for lining up extra layers. It is also hard wearing and can be used repeatedly. Thick, waxed paper is an alternative.

Cutting Knife

You will need a scalpel knife with extra blades to cut your own stencil designs because a very sharp blade is necessary. A blade set at an angle is ideal for cutting arcs and circles.

Cutting Mat

A "self-healing" mat, obtainable from most artist's materials suppliers, is best for cutting out your stencil designs because it will not disintegrate or blunt your blade as quickly as a cutting board would.

Tracing Paper and Graph Paper

You will find that both of these items are extremely useful for copying and reproducing balanced designs.

Now that you have all the materials and equipment you will need, let's start with the first project.

LEFT Cutting materials.

Fun Gift Tag

This is a great project to introduce you to the art of stencilling because it is simple yet effective. Enhance your gifts with a specially stencilled gift tag and delight everyone.

You will need
◊ Painting kit with acrylics
◊ Pad of coloured paper
◊ Hole punch
◊ Curling ribbon

1 We have chosen to stencil a white heart on red paper. Choose an appropriate stencil and paper colour. Measure and cut your paper to approximately 3 × 4in/7.5 × 10cm, and fold it in half along the 2in/5cm line. Decide whether your tag will be horizontal or vertical and punch a hole in the top left-hand corner, leaving enough room for your design.

2 For our practice session we chose to stencil a red heart onto white scrap paper. Put a small amount of paint into a bowl. Dip the bristles of a medium sized brush into the paint and rub off any excess paint on kitchen towel. Your brush should be very dry.

3 Place your stencil design over your scrap paper and hold it with one hand. Hold your stencil brush upright and press it through the stencil cut-out, moving it in a circular motion around the inside edge of the stencil. Continue to build up the colour by moving the brush around the edges. You can do this quite quickly. Try approximately 10 turns but do not let the colour build up in the middle of the cut-out.

4 Practise, practise, practise! If your brush is too wet with paint it may result in a flat, filled-in stencil shape that bleeds around the edges; see the top heart. The brush really does need to be very dry — drier than you would imagine — although the very faint heart has taken this

to the extreme. The heart at the bottom of the photograph, with the shaded edges and light area in the middle, is perfect.

5 Once you are confident with your practice session you can apply exactly the same principle to your pre-cut tag. Use a clean, dry brush. Choose your paint colour and put a little into a clean, dry bowl. Dip the brush in the paint and wipe off the excess. Position the stencil over the tag, hold both firmly in place and build up the colour in a circular motion around the edge of the cut-out.

HANDY HINTS
When you are cutting out your tag, placing your cutting knife along the edge of a ruler offers a more accurate line than cutting with scissors. Use a metal ruler and hold the ruler and paper firmly in place, taking care to keep your fingers out of the way!

Finally, twirl a good length of ribbon and feed it through the hole. Just look at the wonderful gift tags you can easily make yourself. If you want to impress your friends by stencilling the wrapping paper to match too, read on!

All Wrapped Up

Let's take the gift tag project a stage further and decorate some wrapping paper, too. Learn how to repeat your design over a large area.

You will need
◊ Painting kit with acrylics
◊ 1 large sheet of coloured paper

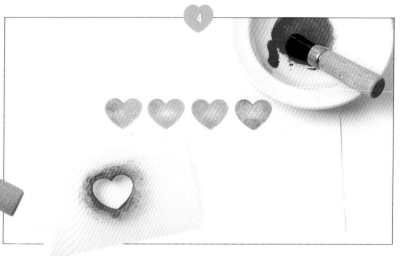

1 We chose to use the same tag stencil as the previous project to make some matching wrapping paper. First, plot some evenly spaced points on a few sheets of scrap paper. Now try some different design layouts.

2 Put some paint in a clean bowl. Dip a clean brush in the paint and wipe off the excess on some kitchen towel. Position your stencil where you want to start on the scrap paper and hold both down firmly. Move your upright brush in a circular motion around the inside edges of the stencil.

3 There are endless ways of building up your own layouts with any stencil. Move the stencil along the grid to see. Try stencilling several different layouts before you decide which you prefer.

4 Sometimes simplest is best. This design is easy to plot, and you don't have to remember to skip any gaps.

6 Position the stencil on the grid. Trace the points of the paper grid on to the stencil using a pencil or permanent ink. This will make it easy for you to position the stencil every time by simply matching the dots so that your alignment will always be perfect.

7 Now stencil your wrapping paper. Get a fresh bowl, brush, paint, and kitchen towel. Place your stencil on the paper and match up the alignment points of the stencil and paper. Hold the stencil and paper firmly and begin.

8 Continue stencilling the whole sheet, remembering to line up the stencil points and paper grid. Compare the stencilled images with each other so that they are roughly the same intensity, but don't try to match them perfectly because their differences add to the appeal of this craft.

The finished wrapping paper with its own matching tag from the first project. A beautiful job, well done!

5 Having chosen your layout, plot the same grid on the real paper. Use very light pencil dots — dark enough for you to be able to use them as a guide to line up your stencil, but not so dark that they detract from your creative efforts.

HANDY HINTS
◊ Do not worry if your stencil images do not fit perfectly within the edges of the paper — when you wrap your gift you may end up cutting off some of the design.

Great Greetings Cards

You can make greetings cards to suit any occasion, but we chose a Christmas card. This project shows you how to use two colours in your design as well as being able to produce several cards at once.

You will need
◊ Painting kit with acrylics
◊ Set of matching cards and envelopes

1 Have at least five plain cards with matching envelopes ready. Make sure that your chosen stencil design is a suitable size for your cards.

2 A two-part stencil gives you an opportunity to use two colours within different parts of the design. Our wreath stencil has separated the green leaves from the red bow and berries. Have ready two bowls, two brushes, two different colours, some kitchen towel and pieces of scrap paper.

3 Try out your first stencil on scrap paper. On a good two-part stencil the first image is cut out and the second image, intact, is drawn in with dotted lines. These dotted lines indicate the rest of the design and are invaluable when you come to line up your second image correctly. Move your brush confidently around the cut-out several times in one direction.

4 Hold the first stencil in place and lift off one corner to peek at your efforts so far. If the image is not strong enough replace the stencil and continue to build up the colour.

5 Now take your second bowl, brush, colour and stencil. Lay the second stencil over the first image. The wreath now shows the bow and berries cut out. The leaves are intact and shown as dotted lines, allowing easy alignment. Stencil your second image.

= 11 =

6 Once you are happy with your practice efforts, have everything to hand to stencil your set of five matching cards.

7 Place your stencil in the appropriate position on the card and hold both firmly. Stencil all five cards in succession with your first image and first colour. Remember to peek at your progress.

8 Carefully position your second image, using the dotted lines for alignment. Hold it down securely to stop it moving.

9 Stencil all five cards with the second image in the second colour. Remember to move your brush in a circular motion in one direction.

You could add a detail of the design to the envelopes for a wonderful finishing touch. Congratulations! You have just completed a production line of hand-decorated cards.

HANDY HINTS

◊ Always use a clean, dry brush for each colour.

◊ Transparent stencils make it easy to line up two or more colours.

◊ You may find a ruler helpful if you cannot easily position your stencil by eye.

◊ When you have very small cut-outs do not try to stencil the edges of each one. You will achieve effective results by simply moving the brush over the cut-outs repeatedly but in only one direction.

A Framed Masterpiece

Make your own stencilled picture to brighten up a plain wall. This project shows you how to use three colours in your design as well as how to build up a border using part of your stencil.

You will need
◊ Painting kit with acrylics
◊ Cutting kit
◊ Sheet of coloured paper
◊ Frame

1 Measure and cut your paper to fit your frame. Make sure they are both a suitable size for the stencil.

2 Our fruit bowl design has been cut in three parts to make it easy to apply three colours. Note the dotted lines for alignment.

3 Choose your paper colour and use an extra piece to experiment with different colour combinations.

4 Practise first! The more you practise, the better your technique will be.

5 Peek to check your efforts and amend them as required.

6 Align your second stencil with your first image. Apply your second colour with a clean brush.

7 Continue with your third colour. Remember to keep your brush dry.

8 Select an easy detail from your design and practise building it into a border.

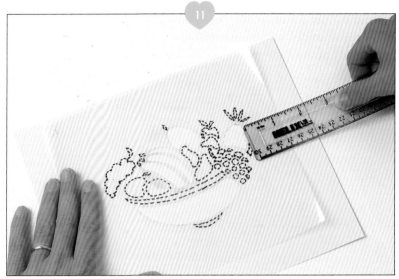

9 Experiment with building up a border by flipping over your stencil and applying your brush through the reverse side.

10 Add another element from the design to see how that looks. There are so many ways of using your stencil.

11 Now decide how best to place your stencil on the real paper. Use a ruler to help you to position it accurately.

12 Stencil your three colours in the usual way, one after the other.

HANDY HINTS
◊ Choose a brush size that is suited to the size of the stencil cut-out.
◊ To select a detail from your stencil mask off the other cut-outs as shown on pages 37—39.

13 A finishing touch in the four corners was all that was needed to complete our picture so that it was ready for framing.

14 Each colour scheme gives a different result. Have fun and experiment.

Magical Mirror

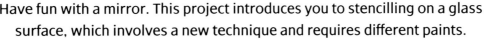

Have fun with a mirror. This project introduces you to stencilling on a glass surface, which involves a new technique and requires different paints.

You will need
◊ Painting kit with ceramic paints
◊ Mirror to decorate
◊ Practice mirror

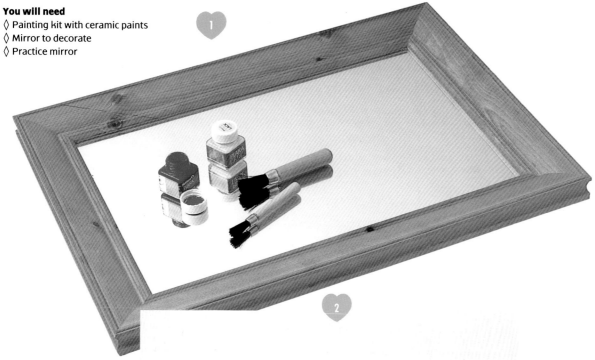

1 Consider the size and shape of your mirror and choose a stencil design accordingly.

2 Practise some design layouts on scrap paper. Note, too, that our shell design has been given some red shading to give it more definition. You will see how to achieve both a highlighting technique (light paint on dark) and a shading technique (dark on light) later on in this project.

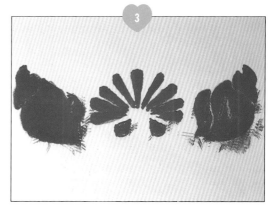

3 Practise your stencilling technique on a spare mirror. Glass is not absorbent, so take care not to use too much paint, or it will smudge.

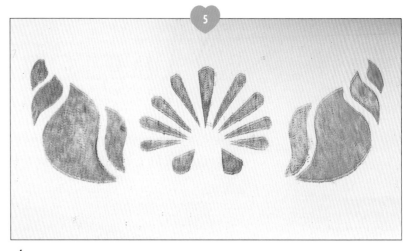

4 Do not use too little paint either. Here the outline of the image is barely distinguishable.

5 This is what you need to aim for. The combination of the properties of this type of paint and this slippery surface means you will need to use more paint and allow it to build up.

6 Now practise stencilling with your first colour.

7 Choose a lighter second colour for the highlighting technique. Hold the brush upright and use an up-and-down motion to stipple your brush into the middle of the cut-out. For the real mirror we use the shading technique.

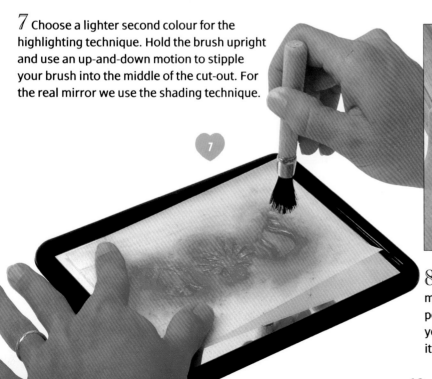

8 When you are ready to move on to the real mirror offer up your stencil to judge the best position. Use your sketches for inspiration. Fix your stencil in place with masking tape to stop it moving about on the slippery surface.

9 Continue your layout with the first colour.

10 For the shaded technique use a darker colour and stipple the edges of the cut-outs with an up and down motion.

A plain mirror has been transformed into a highly individual and decorative piece.

HANDY HINTS
◊ If you need to section off part of your design use masking tape as shown on pages 37–39, or simply hold some spare pieces of paper in place.
◊ Check the drying times of your ceramic paint on the manufacturer's instructions.

Merry Mugs

Stencilled mugs will brighten any kitchen and they also make great gifts. In this project we made a set of three.

You will need
◊ Painting kit with ceramic paints
◊ 3 matching mugs in a plain colour

1 Decide on a design that will suit the shape and size of your mugs. We chose stars.

2 Experiment with colours on a scrap piece of coloured paper. Silver and gold are ideal for stars, and they work well on a blue background.

3 Holding your stencil with masking tape on the curved surface will make stencilling easier.

4 Stencil your first image in the usual way. You may need to stipple the edges to deepen the colour on this dark, non-absorbent surface.

7 As a finishing touch, spatter some silver paint over the mugs. Put more paint on your brush, then pull back the bristles so that they are a little way from the mug and let them flick onto the mug so that small flecks of paint are deposited on the mugs — and everywhere else too! Before you do this, protect anything you do not wish to spatter, including the insides of the mug.

8 Finish off the other mugs also using the spattering technique. It works especially well with the star stencil design, giving the impression of distant galaxies!

Here is your new set of mugs. Treat a friend or yourself!

5 Continue to apply the first image to all three mugs. By the time you have stencilled the third mug, the first mug should be dry enough for you to apply the next image.

6 We have chosen smaller silver stars for the next image. Use a freer and less regimented approach here and build up the small stars into an attractive pattern.

HANDY HINTS
Personalize a mug with a stencilled name to make the perfect gift.

Pots of Gardener's Delight

Stencilling is a wonderful way of transforming plain terracotta flowerpots into a gardener's dream.

You will need
◊ Painting kit with ceramic paints
◊ Any number and size of terracotta pots

1 Select your stencil design according to the size and shape of the pots. You might like to coordinate the colours of the stencil with the plants that are to go into them.

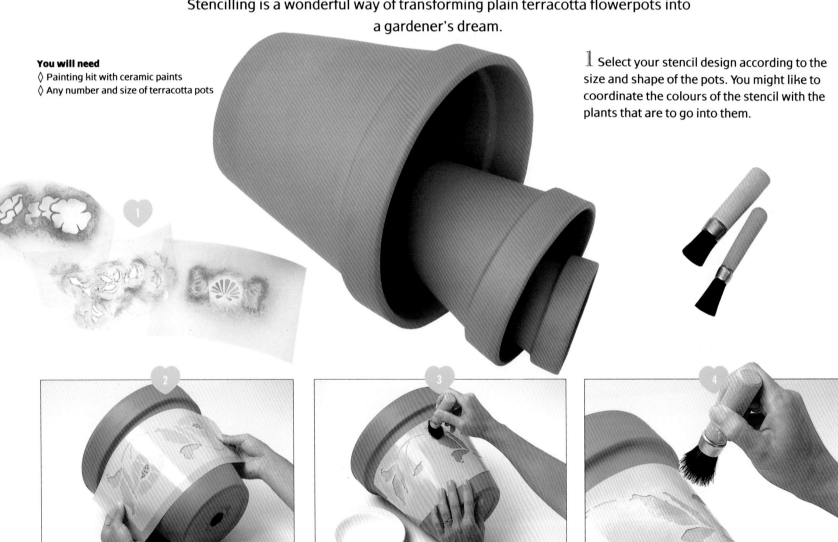

2 Calculate the position of the image by offering up the stencil to the pot. You may need to stretch or squeeze in a repeat pattern.

3 Use masking tape to secure the stencil to the pot, then stencil on your first colour.

4 Stipple the design to add depth before moving the stencil along to continue the first colour.

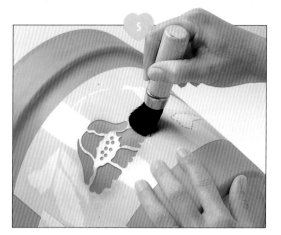

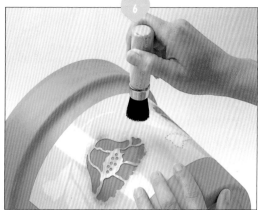

7 The finished design on a large pot shows the effect achieved by the stippling technique.

8 Just look at what you can do. Rather than continuing the design around this pot, we felt that it would work better as a central feature.

A selection of different sized pots and designs.

5 Align your second stencil and apply your second colour.

6 Use the stippling technique again to deepen the edges of the design. Move the stencil around the pot to complete your design.

HANDY HINTS
◊ You may find your stencil more manageable if you trim it to follow the curve of the pot.
◊ This porous surface may require more paint than usual to build up the colour.

Terrific T-Shirt

For your introduction to fabric stencilling, choose a fun stencil and make your own designer T-shirt. Our cat's paw stencil went for a walk all over this one.

You will need
◊ Painting kit with fabric paints
◊ Clean, dry T-shirt in a plain colour

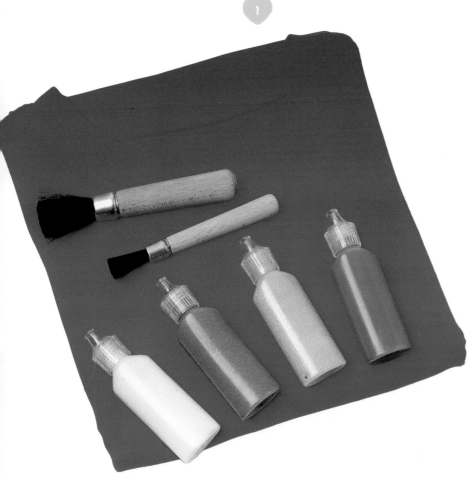

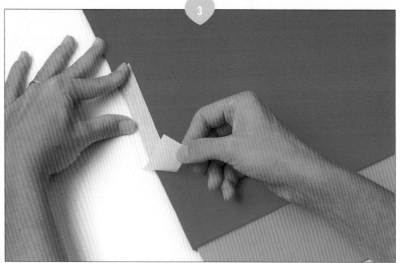

1 Choose a design and a set of colours that will complement your T-shirt.

2 Tape a spare piece of fabric to a smooth surface and practise your stencilling technique on this surface.

3 Once you are happy with your efforts place some scrap paper inside the T-shirt to stop any paint soaking through to the reverse side. Smooth out any creases and tape the T-shirt to a flat surface.

4 Move your stencil design along the front of the T-shirt, around the side and over the back.

5 To give it a sparkle, go over the stencil again with some glitter fabric paint, using the stipple technique.

A plain T-shirt has been transformed into your own designer wear!

HANDY HINTS
◊ Follow the manufacturer's instructions for your chosen fabric paints; you may need to iron over the paints to fix the colours.
◊ Use a gentle stencilling technique to avoid stretching the fabric.

Friendly Floor Covering

Let's move your stencilling talents to the floor. A scatter rug can be decorated to suit any room, and this is a good introduction to working on a larger scale. Remember to apply a varnish to protect the design against inevitable foot traffic.

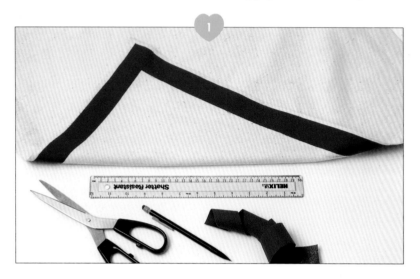

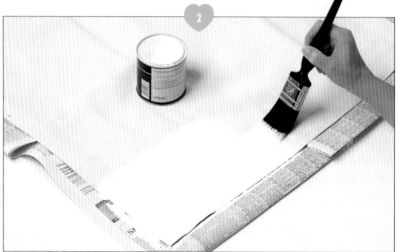

You will need
◊ Painting kit with acrylic paints
◊ Decorator's heavy twill dust sheet or canvas
◊ Iron-on hemming tape or sewing machine
◊ Small tin of matt emulsion paint
◊ Small tin of varnish
◊ Decorator's paint brush

1 Measure and cut your fabric to a manageable size – ours is 2 × 3ft/60 × 90cm. Fold down and seal your edges with hemming tape or use a sewing machine to turn down a hem.

2 Apply a coat of matt emulsion paint to the rug to seal the fabric. Leave to dry. Wash out your brush.

3 Choose a stencil and sketch some possible layouts on scrap paper, remembering to allow for a border line. There are so many ways you can build up designs with your stencil.

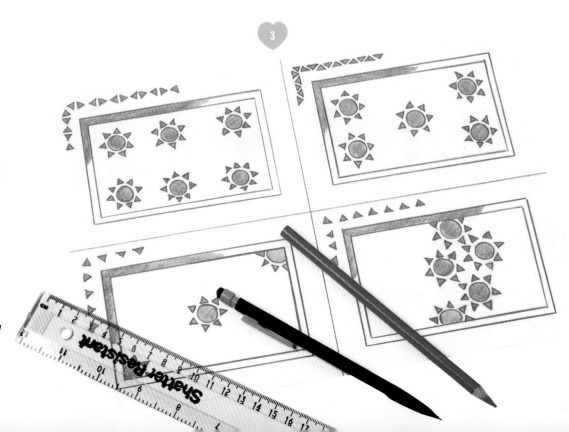

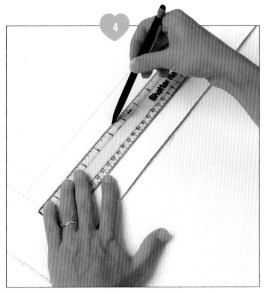

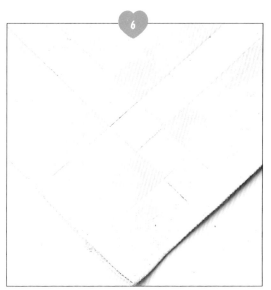

4 Once the paint is dry, measure and mark the border line on your rug. We have marked our pencil lines approximately 2½in/7cm and 4in/10cm from the edge.

5 Apply the masking tape to the pencil lines, leaving a 1½in/3cm gap between.

6 Allow the masking tape to overlap at the corners to create an interesting break in the border.

7 Use a large brush to stencil the 1¼in/3cm gap all around the rug.

8 Remove the masking tape to reveal your border. Refer to your sketches for inspiration and offer up your stencil design to calculate the best spacing. Mark key points.

9 Use your key points to place the stencil and apply your first image over the whole rug. Hold or tape your stencil in place.

10 Line up and apply the second image and continue over the whole rug.

11 On the other side of your border line build up another border with a detail from the stencil. We cut two triangles as a separate stencil for ease of application.

12 Once all the yellow triangles are complete, flip over the stencil and place some upside-down triangles in the design using another colour.

250ml

13 Apply at least two coats of varnish to the whole rug.

A truly friendly floor covering to brighten any room!

HANDY HINTS
◊ Choose a background emulsion colour that will suit the room in which you will place the rug.
◊ When you apply the emulsion and varnish, place some newspaper under the rug to protect your work surface.

Child's Cheerful Chair

This is your first attempt at decorating a piece of furniture. A plain child's stool can be made to look extra special with a stencilled seat and is certain to be a hit!

You will need
◊ Painting kit with acrylics
◊ A new, wooden child's stool, untreated (i.e. not varnished or waxed)
◊ Pair of compasses
◊ Fine-grade sandpaper
◊ Tin of polishing wax

1 Select an appropriate stencil design and a suitable colour scheme. Give the stool a light rub down with fine sandpaper.

2 We decided to stencil our floral design in a circular layout. Start by drawing your circle with the compass on rough paper. Placing an edge of your image on the pencil mark and following the line of the circle will enable you to calculate how close the repeats should be to complete the circle.

3 Apply your first colour. Because you are being creative with this approach, you will be unable to rely on your stencil for the exact spacing of the images, so line them up by eye as well.

4 Apply your second colour, following the line of the circle. Again you will need to line up the stencil by eye as you work around the circumference.

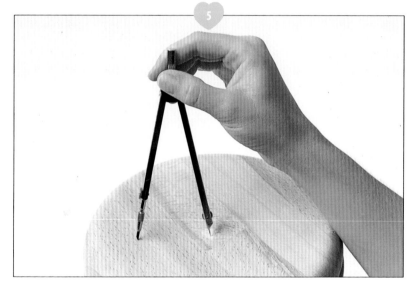

5 Use your compass to mark a light circle on the seat of the stool. Allow enough room between the line and the edge of the stool for your design.

6 Roughly calculate the position of the design and apply your first colour, following the line of the circle.

7 When you have completed the circle with the first colour apply your second image and second colour.

8 Add any finishing touches to suit the piece.

9 Seal your design by applying a coat of wax polish. Buff it up to obtain a deep lustre.

This chair will cheer up any child's day!

A New Lease of Life

You can give any old piece of furniture a new lease of life by adding a stencilled decoration. Resurrect something from your attic and bring it back into your home. We have given an old school desk a pretty, rustic feel.

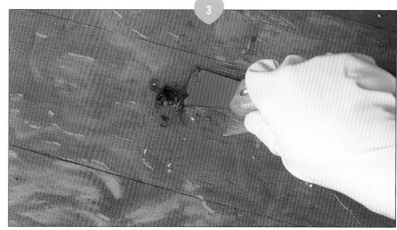

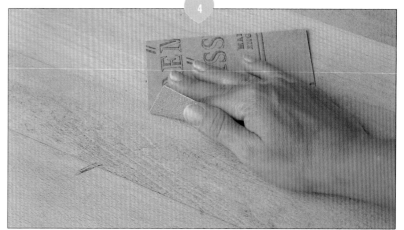

You will need
◊ Painting kit with acrylics
◊ Paint and varnish stripper
◊ Fine-grade sandpaper
◊ Small tin of emulsion paint
◊ Old piece of furniture
◊ Small tin of varnish

1 Almost any old piece of furniture can be used as long as it is in good repair and is well prepared. You will need to remove old paint and varnish.

2 Consider your stencil design and colour scheme and gather the materials you will need.

3 The old varnish on this desk must be removed. Apply the varnish remover and scrape it off. Take care with these materials;

always follow the manufacturer's instructions and wear protective clothing.

4 When it is dry, rub down the surface with fine sandpaper to give a smooth, clean surface. Dust off with a brush or cloth.

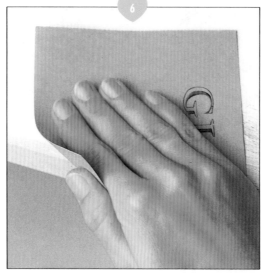

5 Apply a coat of slightly thinned emulsion paint in your chosen background colour. Allow to dry.

6 Rub down the emulsion coat with fine sandpaper to highlight the grain.

7 The combination of the beech wood grain and emulsion give the desired rustic effect.

8 We have chosen a border design for the desk lid. Measure and mark a light guideline so that you can position the stencil correctly.

9 Make sure that the stencil is applied in the correct place and fix it with masking tape.

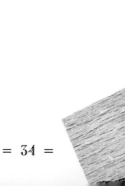

10 Apply the first colour over the whole area.

11 Line up your second stencil and apply all of the second colour.

12 Continue with a third colour.

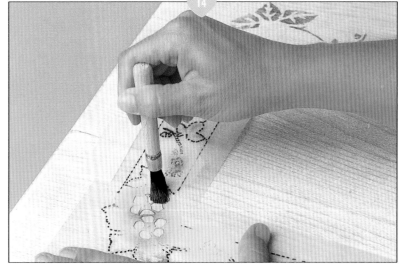

13 A close-up of the completed design reveals that the yellow and green are a little bright for the overall rustic feel of the desk.

14 We stencilled the edges of the design with a little burnt sienna to tone down and add depth to the flowers and leaves.

HANDY HINTS

◊ If your piece of furniture needs only a good clean, use sugar soap.

◊ When you apply the coat of emulsion, paint your strokes in the same direction as the grain.

◊ To give an even more rustic look, lightly sand over your finished design.

15 The result is an "older" and much more interesting design.

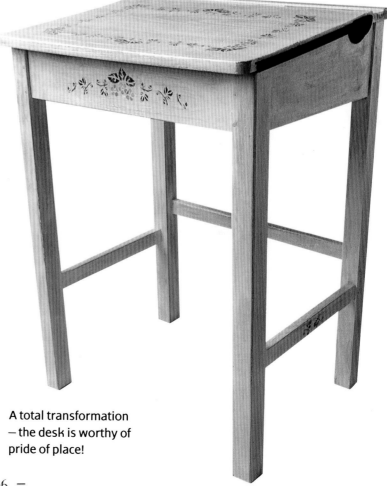

16 Add some finishing touches to suit the piece.

17 Seal in the effect and design with two coats of varnish.

A total transformation – the desk is worthy of pride of place!

Finishing Touches

Stencilling on a wall can bring a room to life. A design above a picture or a plain window can provide the perfect finishing touch, and this project provides an opportunity to coordinate colours with the rest of the room.

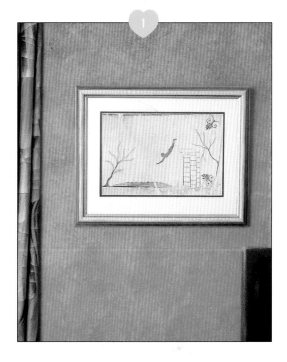

You will need
◊ Painting kit with acrylics
◊ Clean, dry wall
◊ Tape measure
◊ Step ladder

1 The space above this picture is the perfect place for a ribbon stencil.

2 With the picture in place, measure and mark the centre point above it.

3 Centre the stencil above the picture, making certain it is straight, and mark the key points.

4 Remove the picture. Line up your stencil on the key points and fix it in place on the wall with masking tape.

5 We have chosen iridescent gold for this project to complement the gold highlights in the picture frame. Stencil in the usual way.

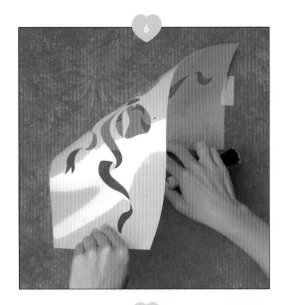

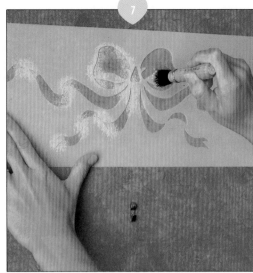

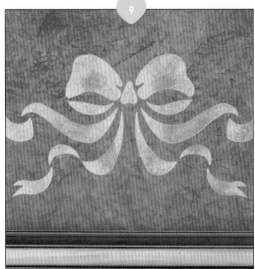

6 A peek at our efforts shows that we need to build up this transparent medium on such a dark background.

7 Heavy stippling is required on key edges of the design.

8 Now that's more like it!

9 Hang your picture back up and admire your handiwork. Does it need anything else?

10 Add a finishing touch by selecting a bit of the design. Tape off the specific areas you want to use.

11 Measure and mark the centre and key points again. Stencil as before.

The stencil has provided an elegant finishing touch for this study.

HANDY HINTS
When you tape off part of your stencil, be sure to add tape to both sides so that the sticky side of the tape does not damage your earlier work.

Designer's Delight

The aim of this project is to design, cut and apply your own border stencil. Your inspiration should come from your own surroundings. We have chosen some lobelia flowers and used them to create a glorious border for a living room.

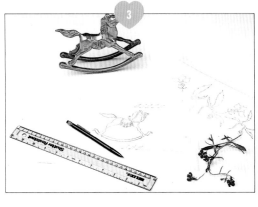

You will need
◊ Cutting kit
◊ Painting kit with acrylics
◊ Appropriate wall space to decorate
◊ Reference material
◊ Coloured pencils
◊ Permanent felt-tip pen

1 Look around for inspiration for a design for your own border stencil.

2 Choose simple objects and practise simplifying the shapes. Look at your chosen object and break it down into sections.

3 Trace the design you like best and hold it in place over graph paper with masking tape. The graph paper will be invaluable in building a straight border. Choose a simple shape from your design to build the outside border.

4 Experiment with different ways of developing your design and also with colours, bearing in mind the room in which you will be stencilling. Make sure that your design is straight by using masking tape to attach your tracing paper to graph paper.

5 Once you have decided on your design and colour scheme, transfer your design to clear polyester drafting film. Use one piece of film for each colour. Fasten your graph and tracing paper to your work surface with masking tape. Place your first piece of film with the frosted side up and hold it in place. Trace a straight line from the graph paper. Now trace all the design shapes of the first colour only. Ensure that the straight line tracing is always aligned with the graph paper.

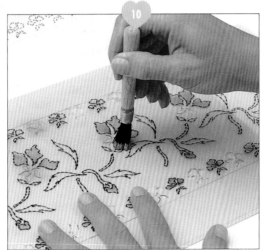

9 Continue in the same way with all three pieces of film. Each piece should have its own shapes cut out to correspond to your planned colour design.

10 Now you can do a trial run with your new stencil on a piece of rough paper. Stencil your first colour, align and stencil your second image and continue with your third.

11 Now you are ready to move to your chosen wall.

6 When you have traced all the shapes for your first colour on to the first piece of film, trace the rest of your design in dotted lines with a permanent felt-tip pen. These dotted lines are essential if you are to align the stencil accurately.

7 On the second piece of film trace all the second colour shapes in a continuous line. Then trace the rest of the design in dotted lines. Continue in the same way for your third colour image.

8 Now you can begin cutting your own stencil, but practise on a spare piece of film first. Use your cutting mat and a sharp blade. Turn the stencil when you come to a corner rather than trying to turn your blade. Cut out the shapes of the continuous line from each piece of film. Do not cut any dotted lines.

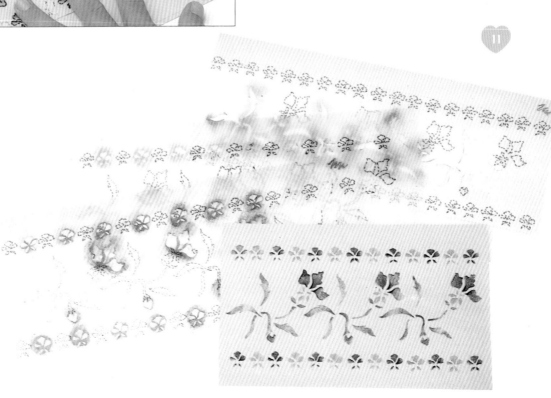

12 This pretty room needs a little something to finish it off.

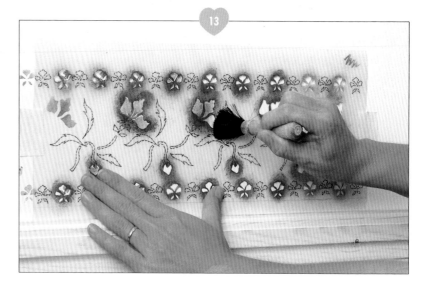

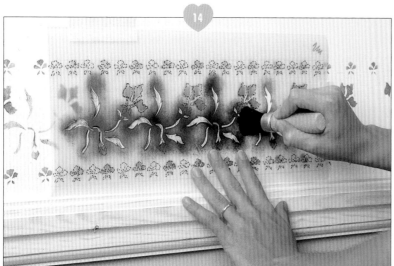

13 Start your first stencil in a relatively inconspicuous place because you will become more confident as you proceed and your technique will improve. This way your best efforts are most visible. After using your first stencil once, move it along and position the repeat by laying your first cut-out over the last image.

14 Once you have completed all of the chosen area with the first colour, proceed with the second colour. Your dotted lines will make alignment simple.

15 Complete the design with the third colour.

16 Put your room back together

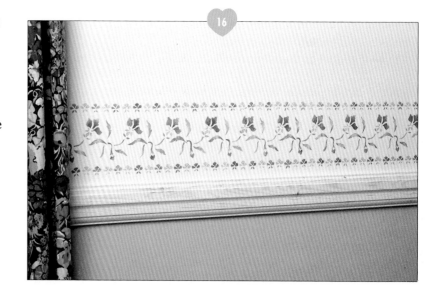

Congratulations! A work of art and a cause for celebration.

HANDY HINTS

◊ The more of your repeat you can fit on to your stencil, the more images you will be able to colour in one go. Remember, though, that the cutting time will be increased.

◊ When you align your repeat by laying a cut-out over a stencilled image, as in Step 13, do not worry if alignment is not exact. You have cut this by hand, so it is bound to be a little different.

◊ Do not use more than three colours.

◊ If your design cuts or tears, it can be easily mended; apply tape on both sides of the tear and trim the excess tape with a blade.

Pattern Library

◊ Magical Mirror

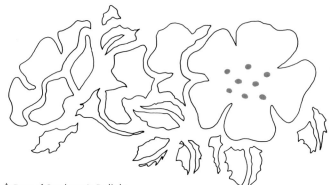

◊ Pots of Gardener's Delight
(Use the shell template from Magical
Mirrors for the small pot) Add pollen
dots by hand

◊ A Framed Masterpiece

◊ Gift Tag *and* All Wrapped Up

◊ Gift Tags *and* Merry Mugs

◊ Designer's Delight

◊ Pots of Gardener's Delight

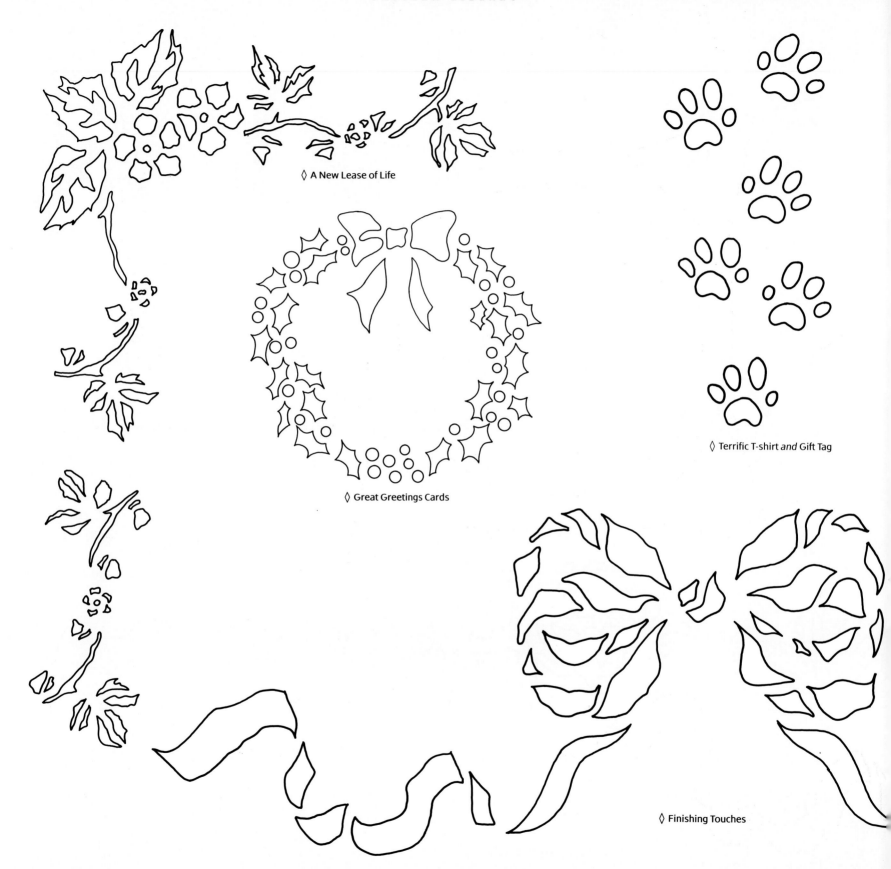

◊ A New Lease of Life

◊ Terrific T-shirt *and* Gift Tag

◊ Great Greetings Cards

◊ Finishing Touches

◊ Child's Cheerful Chair

◊ Friendly Floor Covering

Acknowledgements

The publishers would like to thank the following for their help in the preparation of this book:

The Bermuda Collection
Special thanks to Yukiko Tanimizu
4 Smithbrook Kilns, Cranleigh, Surrey GU6 8JJ, UK

Eurostudio (for supplying some of the stencils)
Unit 4, Southdown Industrial Estate, Southdown Rd,
Herts AL5 1PW, UK

What Not Antiques (for supplying the child's stool
and mirror)
56 Smithbrook Kilns, Cranleigh, Surrey, UK

Liquitex UK (for supplying artist's acrylic paints)
Ampthill Rd, Bedford MK2 9RS, UK

A. S. Handover Limited (for supplying stencilling
equipment)
Angel Yard, Highgate High Street, London N6 5JU, UK